What Readers THINK, FEEL, AND SAY—

"Running a Juice Stand is a delightful tale that weaves a timeless message about business morals with a story of a grandfather passing on his knowledge to another generation. As an architect with a firm that has locations in seven cities, the message rang particularly true. The easy manner in which the story flows and the likeable characters make the book a quick read and reinforces the importance of the 6 E's. I heartily endorse this book to anyone who runs, or wants to run, a successful business."

TRUDI G. HUMMEL, AIA
MANAGING PRINCIPAL, GOULDEVANS ASSOCIATES

"Congratulations on your new book, *Running a Juice Stand: The 6 E's of Wise Management.* An excellent primer for any and all who seek to manage and/or lead a community college or any other 'outcome oriented' organization. I am delighted to endorse this useful and extremely well written handbook."

John E. Roueche, PROFESSOR AND DIRECTOR
SID W. RICHARDSON REGENTS CHAIR, THE UNIVERSITY OF TEXAS AT AUSTIN,
COLLEGE OF EDUCATION

"Don Schoening has taken us back to the managerial basics of any effective and efficient organization by successfully squeezing, selling, and serving the real juice—the 6 E's. A reflection of life's lessons that's an easy read for young and old."

Jerry R. Lewis, Ed.D., PROFESSOR OF EDUCATIONAL LEADERSHIP
NORTHERN ARIZONA UNIVERSITY IN YUMA, YUMA, ARIZONA

"In a time when the world seems complex, the basics of business and management are so simple. *Running a Juice Stand* clearly outlines what every individual business and organization can take to heart and become successful."

Mark S. Watson, CITY ADMINISTRATOR
CITY OF YUMA, ARIZONA

"A readable gem that is useful in building writing skills, ethical reasoning as well as critical and creative thinking with adult learners."

Kevin Mann, PROFESSOR OF ESL, ADULT EDUCATOR
ARIZONA WESTERN COLLEGE

"Thank you so much for giving me the opportunity to read your book! I would love to purchase this book for my classroom. I believe the children can really learn a lot from Jimmy! I sure did!"

Mackenzie McCully, TEACHER OF THE YEAR, YUMA COUNTY SCHOOL DISTRICT
DESERT MESA ELEMENTARY SCHOOL, YUMA, ARIZONA

"I had a staff person asking to borrow the book before I even had a chance to read it! The connection of its principles through concrete examples makes this book accessible for all ages."

Susan Klein Rothschild, MSW
DIRECTOR OF CLARK COUNTY FAMILY SERVICES, LAS VEGAS, NEVADA

"*Running a Juice Stand* is a refreshingly easy to read book whose principles as outlined by the 6 E's are central to life's successes. It also transcends non-generational boundaries while framing the characteristics of good management."

Rufus Glasper, Ph.D., CPA, CHANCELLOR
MARICOPA COMMUNITY COLLEGES, PHOENIX, ARIZONA

"*The 6 E's of Wise Management* is a truly enjoyable book. The down-to-earth examples of managing a juice stand provide meaningful guidelines that can be used at all levels of management. Managers working in small business and those in complex health systems will benefit from incorporating the 6 E's into their daily practice. The lively story makes it a pleasure to read for managers of all skill levels and ages."

Mary Woods, DIRECTOR, BUSINESS DEVELOPMENT
CARSON TAHOE REGIONAL HEALTHCARE, CARSON CITY, NEVADA

"*Running a Juice Stand* is a great read for all school administrators. From our daily perspectives there are lessons to be remembered and also introduced to our classrooms. From the lesson planning book to the principals office this little book has great teaching moments throughout. Running a Juice Stand truly can be used K–12 and is supported by the Arizona School Administrators Superintendents Division."

Tim Foist, SUPERINTENDENT
PRESIDENT OF ASA SUPERINTENDENTS DIVISION 2005-06

RUNNING

A JUICE STAND:

The 6E's of Wise Management

By Don E. Schoening, Ph.D.

RUNNING A JUICE STAND:
THE 6 E'S OF WISE MANAGEMENT

Don Schoening, Ph.D.

Dedicated to my friends and colleagues in education whose support and enthusiasm for the 6 E's stimulated me to write this book.

Credits:

Layout. *Jose Renteria, Media Arts Student*
Illustrations. *Marco Rodriguez & Josue Soto, Media Arts Students*
Project Manager. *Professor Brad Pease, M.F.A.*
Cover Photo (inside lemons, front cover). *Professor Pete Self, M.A.*
Cover Design. *Ike Erb, Creative Manager, College Publications*

Redi-Gro Publishing Company
11390 E. Via Canada
Yuma, AZ 85367

www.redigropublishing.com

Notice of Rights:

Running a Juice Stand: The 6 E's of Wise Management
Don Schoening, Ph.D.

ISBN 0-9766481-0-5

Printed in the United States of America.

For more information about Running a Juice Stand Books, Learning Materials, Study Guides and Organizational Consulting:

1-928-305-9246
info@redigropublishing.com

TABLE OF CONTENTS

Running a Juice Stand or the 6 E's of Wise Management was written primarily to help managers of organizations focus on what is really vital to success. The book applies to organizations as simple as a juice stand to complex national or international institutions.

My educational career began as a seventh grade teacher and, with many stops along the way, ended as a college president. Throughout my career, each time I interviewed for a promotion, questions arose about leadership, management, and organizational success. I began to focus my attention on successful organizations and how a leader created a climate for growth, improved performance, and vision.

As I expressed my viewpoints in response to questions about leadership and management, people became interested in a model that I used for decision-making. Over a period of time the model evolved from 2 or 3 E's to a 6 E model. Running a Juice Stand demonstrates the model in practical terms that can be universally understood.

Running a Juice Stand can be used as an introductory tool for managers or employees entering an organization to explore core values during organizational orientation. Seasoned executives, when they read the book, are reminded to return to the basics of organizational success. Once entering employees and experienced executives read the book, they have an opportunity to share a common set of success indicators.

As people I knew read Running a Juice Stand, a secondary target audience began to emerge. People began to share the book with their children and grandchildren outside the work place. The 6 E's for organizational success were values that they wanted to share with family and friends.

Perhaps, rather unexpectedly, the book applies to people and organizations at all levels. Children, teachers, parents, and grandparents can identify with the operation of a juice stand and the lessons Jimmy learned.

Finally, Running a Juice Stand was written to be read and enjoyed. The book presents a universal plan for organizational success. In the end, if you discover the 6 E's Jimmy learned, with help from his grandfather, you can utilize them successfully with your family, career, business or organization.

TAKING OVER

Jimmy's older brother, Frank, was going to junior high school next year and offered to turn over his summer juice business to Jimmy. For three summers, Frank had sold a blended combination of several orange and lemon juices along a frontage road off a freeway exit. The lot for the stand had been purchased years before by Frank and Jimmy's great-grandfather.

Frank's customers had been cyclists, walkers, and shoppers. Frank explained to Jimmy that people of all ages enjoyed the juice. Frank opened at 10:00 a.m. and closed promptly at 2:00 p.m. Frank averaged about twenty dollars a day all summer. The agreement Frank had with his parents was to save half of the money for college. Frank used the additional money for a supplement to his basic allowance.

Each year Jimmy's grandfather organized the family to pick lemons and oranges from their groves. Picking was hard work but everyone had fun working together. Everyone then helped to squeeze the juice from the ripe

*Jimmy's grandfather organized his family
to help with the juice stand*

lemons and oranges. The juice was then frozen for use in the summer. The day ended with a big family picnic in the neighborhood to celebrate the harvest.

Needless to say, Jimmy was anxious to get started making real money. He had big plans to become wealthy or at least rich. Frank carefully explained to Jimmy that his juice was a measured blend of two types of oranges and two different kinds of lemons. Frank showed Jimmy how to carefully blend the four juices. He helped Jimmy repaint their sign which now read, "Jimmy's Juice Stand." Jimmy felt proud to have his name on the juice stand.

Everything went well. Frank introduced his younger brother, Jimmy, to his customers. After a week, Frank left Jimmy on his own. He followed Frank's instructions to the

Jimmy mixing juice without much care
about the proper blend

letter. He opened promptly at 10:00 and closed at 2:00.
Jimmy measured out four equal portions of orange and
lemon juice each morning and sold most of his juice by
2:00 each day so he had very little waste.

One morning he was late so he quickly mixed his
four juices together without much care. The juice sold
fine, although a few older shoppers thought the juice had
a bitter taste. Jimmy decided that Frank's concern with
carefully measuring orange and lemon juice was not
really necessary and took a lot of extra time and effort.
Jimmy felt good that he had found an easier way to do
business and still make the same profit. Jimmy quickly
mixed the four juices without measuring portions.
Although business began to decline a little each day,

Jimmy blamed his downturn on lack of customers and more people drinking sodas and juice from nearby stores. Still, Jimmy was very discouraged. Jimmy decided to ask Frank for advice. Frank took one taste of juice and frowned with a bitter expression on his face. "Your juice tastes terrible. What happened?" Jimmy hated to tell Frank that he was now paying little attention to the mixture of juices. He reluctantly admitted to his older brother that he was not carefully measuring portions before he blended his juice every morning.

Frank said, "It's time for you to go see Grandfather for advice. He will share his secret model for success." Jimmy's grandfather was chairman of the board for National Beverage Corporation. Jimmy's father was president of the company.

Jimmy went to Teri, his grandfather's assistant, to ask to see his grandfather. Teri asked if he had an appointment because his grandfather was extremely busy. Jimmy felt very downcast because he had not even thought to make an appointment. As he turned to leave, Teri called him back saying his grandfather had arranged for him to come right in, as much as he was a fellow businessman.

Jimmy explained everything that had happened. He told about his initial success but also about how business had now begun to go downhill. Jimmy's grandfather looked thoughtfully over his glasses at Jimmy. He asked, "Have you changed anything you are doing now that you weren't doing when your business was going well?" Jimmy explained about changing the blended mix of two types of orange juices and two types of lemon juices. Jimmy's grandfather sighed and turned to a large poster behind his desk, which simply said, '6 E's.' "Jimmy," his grandfather explained, "you have made the typical business person's mistake. You violated one of the 6 E's. By not paying attention to the recipe and mix given to you by Frank, you tried to sell a product that was not quality controlled. You now have a juice that is no longer considered excellent by your customers."

Jimmy begins to learn about the 6E's

Jimmy's eyes were wide with a mixture of fear and disappointment. "But Grandfather," Jimmy blurted out, "now that I have violated a principle of the 6 E Model, what can I do?" "You must discover this for yourself," Grandfather said. As Jimmy left his grandfather's office, he was puzzled and confused.

As he walked home, he studied his first three weeks of business experience. All of a sudden, a light came on in Jimmy's mind. He realized that the reason he and Frank had sold so much juice was because of the excellence of the product. The stand's customers had grown used to a "quality-controlled" juice, to use his grandfather's words.

Jimmy went back to a carefully prepared mix of four blended juices. People noticed the improvement and nodded approval when they tasted the juice. In a little while business was back to normal. He wrote in his little blue notebook "Excellence: Have a good product to sell."

Excellence:

Have a good
product to sell

P.s. maintain quality
control.

BEING FAIR

As the summer went on, Jimmy felt more and more confident about running his stand. Now that he understood having a good product to sell was one of his grandfather's 6 E's, he carefully measured his blends of juice so his quality was always consistent and, therefore, excellent.

Sometimes he thought about the other E's in his grandfather's 6 E Model. But since everything was going well, he continued his stand's business as usual. One afternoon after his younger sister's, Elizabeth's, birthday party, he questioned his grandfather about the other E's in his success model. His grandfather smiled and said, "We businessmen need our personal time to enjoy life." Jimmy's discussion was interrupted when his mother placed a large piece of chocolate cake with ice cream in front of Jimmy and his grandfather.

During the summer, many of Jimmy's friends stopped to visit. His friends played all day while Jimmy was hard at work during the middle of each weekday. At first they enjoyed stopping by just to talk. As time went on, they grew tired of waiting for Jimmy while he sold cups of juice to his many customers. Jimmy sometimes felt sorry

Jimmy learned that the juice buisness took time away from his friends

for himself because he was tied down to regular business hours and could not break away to play.

As fewer and fewer of his friends came by, Jimmy came up with a way of encouraging his friends to visit at the juice stand. Jimmy began to give his friends a free cup of juice. His idea worked very well because each day his friends stopped by for a few minutes. Once in a while, his customers had to wait while Jimmy visited with his

Jimmy's friends sometimes became more important than his customers

friends. Jimmy's stand continued to do quite well so he gave little attention to his customers' concerns.

As more and more of Jimmy's friends wanted free juice, he realized that giving away free juice reduced the number of cups he was selling and also his profit. Jimmy did not want to lose his friends so he was reluctant to quit giving away free juice.

Jimmy noticed that some of his senior shoppers in the afternoon sometimes did not always drink all of their juice. Jimmy came up with an idea to solve his problem. He purchased smaller cups for his afternoon customers. His morning customers continued to receive their juice in large paper cups. Jimmy's afternoon customers got less juice in smaller cups. Jimmy kept giving free juice to his friends by using the juice saved in the afternoon. Jimmy paid little attention to complaints about the difference in cup size from morning as compared to afternoon.

Jimmy prepared the same amount of juice each day but sales began to drop drastically. Afternoon sales accounted for his largest reduction but surprisingly even morning profits went down. One good thing had happened, however; Jimmy had more friends than ever.

Unfortunately, business became so bad that he finally asked his father for help. He explained everything to his dad. His father responded, "I think I know what is causing sales to go down but you really need to see Grandfather for his wisdom."

Jimmy felt very small in the large leather chair in front of his grandfather's huge oak desk. His grandfather listened carefully as he explained about trying to keep customers and please his friends. Jimmy's grandfather clasped his hands as he swiveled toward the large poster behind his desk that read, "6 E's."

It seemed like forever before his grandfather finally turned back to face Jimmy. "Equity," he said. "You have an equity problem." His grandfather's expression was

Jimmy discovers the meaning of equity

so grave that Jimmy simply murmured, "Thank you, Grandfather."

Jimmy had no idea what his grandfather had meant by equity. On the way home, he decided to ride his bicycle to his grandmother's house. His grandmother, as usual, was glad to see Jimmy. After he finished chocolate chip cookies and cold milk, he asked his grandmother what equity meant. She turned to a bookcase and pulled down a large dictionary. Jimmy leafed through the pages until he found the word, "equity." One definition had to do with the value of property above the total amount owed on a mortgage. The other definition looked more promising. It simply said, "fairness or impartiality." He thanked his grandmother and headed home in deep thought as he pedaled slowly along.

Jimmy knew his product was excellent so that was not a problem. His grandfather had said his problem had been with equity. How had he been unfair? The more he thought about equity and fairness, the more Jimmy began to understand that by trying to buy friends with free juice, he had been unfair to his regular customers. He realized that giving afternoon customers a smaller cup for the same price was also not right.

When he reached home, he explained to his mother what he had learned about equity. "You have learned both a new word and a good business lesson," she said. "But Mother," Jimmy asked, "how can I keep all my friends? They will be unhappy when they no longer get a cup of juice for free." "Jimmy," his mother explained, "a businessman must decide how he can solve his problems for himself."

The next day he explained to his friends about equity, fairness, and impartial treatment. He said he was sorry he could not give away any more free juice. His friends were disappointed, but after awhile his closest friends began to return. Jimmy realized that you can keep your best friends without giving away your product. Those who came by only for a free drink of juice that summer didn't matter as much as his closer more loyal buddies. By the end of the month his business had begun to return to normal. He wrote in his little blue notebook "Equity: Be fair to all your customers." Jimmy carefully underlined the word "<u>all</u>."

People returned when Jimmy treated everyone fairly

When school began in the fall, Jimmy closed his shop and hurriedly put away his equipment and supplies. He was very pleased with all he had learned that summer. Jimmy knew that a good business needed an excellent product. He understood that equity meant that successful businesses treated all their customers fairly.

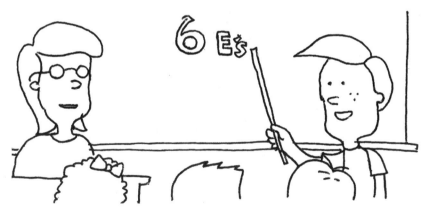

*Jimmy shares what he learned about
excellence and equity*

Miss Largent, his fifth grade teacher, asked him to share what he did over the summer. Jimmy explained how he had operated his juice stand over the past summer. Miss Largent was very pleased when the class questioned Jimmy about his experience and how important excellence and equity were to operating a juice stand. The class wanted to know about the other four E's in his grandfather's 6 E's of success. Jimmy said he did not know all the 6 E's yet but that his grandfather used them to run National Beverage Corporation. He told the class that his brother, Frank, and his dad and uncles learned the 6 E's by running the family juice stand. Miss Largent said she would ask the sixth grade teacher next year to be sure and let Jimmy share the remaining E's for success.

When the school year was over, Jimmy started thinking about opening his juice stand for the second summer. Business started slowly; Jimmy wondered what was wrong. He noticed that some of his customers rode on or walked on by. Business continued to get worse. He became quite concerned "but what could be wrong?" he thought. He had an excellent product and he treated each customer equitably. Finally he asked his brother, Frank, if he could stop by again and help discover what was causing buisness to go down.

Jimmy's brother, Frank, thinks the stand looks rundown and shabby

Frank took one look and shook his head. "Our stand looks rundown and shabby," Frank said. "The paint is weathered, weeds are growing everywhere, and the garbage can lids are broken." He said, "What you need to do is visit with Grandfather and seek his advice."

As Jimmy pedaled his bike up to National Beverage Corporation headquarters where his grandfather's offices were, he noticed for the first time how nice the buildings

Jimmy notices the appearance of National Beverage Corporation

looked and how neat and clean the lawns and parking areas were. He let his grandfather's assistant know he was here for his appointment. Jimmy was glad he had learned to make appointments. As he settled back in the large leather sofa to wait, he thought about how his shabby stand looked and how impressive National Beverage Corporation looked.

When Jimmy explained about sales falling off and his brother Frank's concern about the look of the stand, his grandfather seemed to wait forever before he spoke. Jimmy's grandfather finally nodded his head and said, "I will be by this Saturday afternoon to look things over."

Jimmy was concerned that his grandfather did not share another of the 6 E's of success, but he decided to wait until Saturday to ask about another E.

On Saturday afternoon after 2:00 when the stand was closed, Jimmy's grandfather and his facilities manager came by with a truck. "Follow Ed's directions carefully because he has a lot of experience with successful businesses," said Grandfather. Ed soon had Jimmy cutting weeds, replacing wood, painting, and spreading gravel. Jimmy worked very hard and grew very tired but he kept on working as Ed directed. Ed smiled and patted him on the head as he drove off. Jimmy waited for his grandfather.

Jimmy's grandparents appreciate the effort to improve the business

When Jimmy's grandfather returned with his grandmother, they all stepped back from the stand. They admired the fresh paint, the graveled lot, and the neat appearance of the stand. Grandmother smiled knowingly and said, "Never forget the importance of appearance." Jimmy was very tired but very proud. He thought, "Sometimes hard work makes you feel good."

Effort brings customers back

On the way to dinner, Grandfather shared with Jimmy that he now knew about another of the 6 E's. Jimmy was puzzled because he really did not know what another of Grandfather's E's was. "The E will come to you if you listen carefully," Grandfather said. Jimmy's customers noticed how nice the stand looked and complimented Jimmy on how much work he had put into improvements. One customer mentioned that effort is its own reward. All of a sudden, a light came on in his head. Jimmy realized that the E stood for effort.

He wrote in his little blue notebook "Effort: Work hard at your business."

GAINING EXPERIENCE | 4

Business improved each week of Jimmy's second summer of running the stand. He understood the need for good solid effort in keeping his stand in good shape. He remembered the lesson he had learned about being careful to blend his juice according to the instructions so his product was excellent. Jimmy was careful to treat each customer fairly so he knew the E that stood for equity was important.

About midsummer many of the supplies, including cups, napkins and straws, needed to be replaced. Each week he usually asked one of his friends to pick up cups at the grocery store. Jimmy usually bought straws and napkins whenever he ran out. Everything ran as usual. His customers were happy and kept buying juice, although they seemed to wonder about the different size and shape of the cups Jimmy used to serve the juice. Sometimes he used plastic cups and sometimes paper cups. The napkins were often different colors and straws were sometimes unavailable at the store. During one week Jimmy's friend, Donald, bought cups that were larger than usual but that was not a problem because Jimmy always measured out the correct amount and explained to his customers about the cups being bigger. His sales were holding steady so he was pleased with himself. Once in a while he wondered about the other E's on his grandfather's wall but since things were going well, they were probably not as important as excellence, equity, and effort. Jimmy thought to himself "Maybe 3 E's are all that are necessary."

Jimmy thought 3E's might be all he needed

Jimmy closed his stand after his second summer. He had not learned about another E for success but when he asked his grandfather about the remaining 3 E's, he just smiled. "Jimmy, it may be that you don't need the other E's. We will see."

The last thing Jimmy had to do was total up his money from sales. A strange thing had happened during the summer. During the first part of the summer, he had sold less juice but had made more profit. During the last part of the season, he sold more than the first part of the summer but he had made less money. Jimmy thought this was puzzling.

Jimmy learns about cost, sales and profit

At the picnic held by National Beverage Corporation to honor all the employees, his Uncle Barry, the company business manager, asked him how his summer had been.

"Fine," he said, "but I made less money in the second half of the summer although I sold more juice." "Come by my office on Monday," Uncle Barry said, "and bring your records."

When Jimmy arrived in his uncle's office, Jimmy sheepishly took out his shoebox of receipts and his blue notebook where he had carefully written down the amount of each day's sales for the summer. Uncle Barry's fingers seemed to fly over the computer keyboard as he added up the total amount of the summer's sales by the month. He then arranged the receipts for purchases in neat stacks and added them together, also.

Uncle Barry looked solemnly at a computer printout he had prepared. "Jimmy, you did a good job of keeping the amount of your sales and all your receipts. Everything was accurate," he said. He added that Jimmy had some inventory control and purchasing problems. "But inventory and purchasing do not begin with an E,' Jimmy said.

Uncle Barry helps Jimmy learn about inventory control and purchasing

Uncle Barry said, "Here, take this information into your grandfather. Maybe he can help you." He led Jimmy down the hall where his grandfather met him in the office. He looked over the computer printout Uncle Barry had given him.

Once again his grandfather turned back to the 6 E's on the wall. "Efficiency," he said. "Your profit went down because of lack of efficiency." Jimmy's grandfather carefully explained that businessmen had a sacred trust to produce an excellent product at a low cost for people. "When you ran out of supplies of cups, napkins, and straws in midsummer, you paid attention to sales but not to expenses, so your business became less efficient." Jimmy

Jimmy and Grandfather share the sacred trust of efficiency and profit

thanked his grandfather and headed back to his Uncle Barry's office. "Grandfather says I have a problem with one of the 6 E's called efficiency," Jimmy said.

"Jimmy," his Uncle Barry smiled and said, "Let's see what we can do." They quickly totaled the amount of the cups, napkins, straws, and cleaning supplies Jimmy would need for next summer. Jimmy called three restaurant supply distributors that his Uncle had suggested.

Jimmy learns about bulk purchasing

He gave them the list of supplies he needed. He waited in his Uncle's office while each one called back with a quote for his stand's supplies for the next summer. Jimmy selected the bid that was the lowest for the items he needed. The next morning, Jimmy and his uncle stopped at the distribution center and Jimmy paid for his supplies. "Now I know about inventory control and bulk purchasing," Jimmy told his uncle. He remembered his grandfather's explanation about a businessman's responsibility of sacred trust to sell an excellent product at a reasonable cost.

Jimmy felt good because he could still sell his juice at the same price next summer and make a good profit. He wrote in his blue notebook "Efficiency: Watch your costs."

Jimmy was happy to begin sixth grade. It was fun to be back at school with all his friends. One day he saw his fifth grade teacher, Miss Largent, in the hallway. She asked him how his summer had been and if he had learned any more of his grandfather's 6 E's. Before he could respond, his friends who wanted to play soccer interrupted him. After school he stopped by to tell Miss Largent about the new E's, effort and efficiency. Jimmy was disappointed that she was busy with some students taking a test.

Jimmy was disappointed that he had not been able to share the new E's

The next day his new teacher, Mr. Baxter, asked Jimmy to stay in the classroom during the lunch hour. Jimmy worried all morning that he had done something wrong. Mr. Baxter asked Jimmy to walk with him to the lunchroom. On the way, he said, "Miss Largent would like to bring her fifth grade class to homeroom with our class. We are inviting your grandfather to talk about the 6 E's." Jimmy felt very pleased to have his grandfather come to both classes.

His grandfather looked very distinguished in his suit and tie. Jimmy felt very important as he introduced his grandfather to the fifth and sixth grade classes. His

Grandfather thanked teachers when he came to speak at Jimmy's school

grandfather first thanked the students for being there. He then turned to Miss Largent and thanked her for all she had taught Jimmy in fifth grade. He laughed when he said, "That was a difficult job." The children laughed with him as Jimmy blushed. "Seriously, " his grandfather spoke, "the most important people in our lives may be our teachers. Thank you for all you do." His grandfather smiled at Miss Largent and Mr. Baxter.

Jimmy's grandfather talked about National Beverage Corporation. He told the class that his company had been built on the 6 E's. He went on to talk about the wonderful people who worked for the company. He explained that people make a difference. He then asked if there were any questions. Several students in Jimmy's class raised their hands. "Jimmy told us about excellence and equity, but what are the other E's?" Maria, Jimmy's classmate, asked.

Jimmy's grandfather surprised everyone by introducing Jimmy to share the new E's he had learned over the summer. Jimmy explained how he had let his stand run down and how much work and effort he had to invest in painting, spreading gravel, and repairing his business. He went on to share what he had learned about managing expenses so the business could be efficient and sell an excellent juice. He explained that efficiency led to a product that was more affordable to everyone which was equity. His grandfather clapped his hands when Jimmy finished and all the students joined in the applause.

Jimmy's grandfather stood up and thanked the class for its attention and turned to leave. Jimmy's best friend, Don, blurted out, "But what about the other 2 E's?" Jimmy's grandfather's eyes twinkled as he said, "The seeking of answers is part of the mystery of education. Maybe next year Jimmy will know all of the 6 E's."

As the weather turned warm in the spring, Jimmy was anxious to open his stand. He knew about excellence, equity, efficiency, and effort. Jimmy had two summers of experience and he had a great new idea he wanted to try.

Jimmy felt very good with 4E's

With some of his profit, Jimmy went to the big department store near his stand and bought ten cases of juice in bottles. It was not quite the same as his own juice, but it did taste pretty good. He put the bottles of juice in a cooler with ice and put up a sign for sale--bottled juice. His customers saw the juice but they preferred the fresh juice Jimmy's family had produced. Jimmy was disappointed that he had ten cases of juice he could not sell.

One day as he was taking the juice out of the cooler when he was closing the stand, the label came off the bottle. The next day he pasted a handwritten label with "Jimmy's Juice" on the bottle. A customer saw the bottle and quickly bought it. Jimmy was excited that he had found a new way to expand his sales and increase his profit.

Jimmy was excited that he could expand sales and profit without a lot of additional effort

One day the produce manager from the Super Buy Store came by to buy a cup of juice. He complimented Jimmy on how good his juice tasted. He looked surprised when he noticed the bottles of juice with Jimmy's labels on them.

The very next afternoon Jimmy's grandfather's big black car pulled into his driveway while Jimmy was playing basketball. Grandfather challenged Jimmy to a game of horse. Grandfather was slow but had a good eye for shooting. After the game, Jimmy's grandfather mentioned that his sales representative stopped by for a visit at a super discount department store. "The produce manager was concerned that you were selling their juice under your label. Is this true, Jimmy?" he said. Jimmy explained that he had not been able to sell the juice until he put his label on the bottle.

Jimmy and his grandfather share buisness ideas

Jimmy's grandfather said, "Let me ask you a question. Do you think people are buying the bottled juice because they expect the same juice as you sell in your stand?" "But Grandfather, I didn't tell them it was our juice," Jimmy said. His grandfather paused and then asked again, "Jimmy, do you think your customers expected to get your juice?" Jimmy realized his grandfather was right but he felt like being stubborn. "They should have known it wasn't my juice if it was in a bottle," he said but he knew he was losing the argument.

Grandfather looked stern as he said, "You used your name on the label to sell a different product and that is really a problem." "What should I do?" Jimmy asked. "That's for you to decide, Jimmy," he said. "Think about what you have done and how it affected people and do the right thing." Jimmy knew that this was not the time to ask about another E. As he thought through his problem, he realized that he had not been honest with his customers and with the Super Buy Store from which he had purchased the bottled juice.

Jimmy wrote a letter of apology to his customers that he placed on his stand and explained what had happened. Several people said an apology was hard to make but they appreciated honesty. Jimmy wrote a letter to the produce manager, which he showed to his father. His father read the letter and suggested that they take it by personally the next day.

When they got to the produce manager's office, he took them to the general manager, Mr. Hall. Mr. Hall said hello to Jimmy's father and shook Jimmy's hand. He read the letter of apology from Jimmy and rocked back in his chair. "I wanted to meet you because I have known your grandfather for many years. National Beverage Corporation is known over the country for its high standards and ethical conduct. Your grandfather once told me that honesty and ethics are the backbone of business. A company has only its good name and reputation. You learned early on in your life about business ethics." As Jimmy and his father left the department store, he turned to his father and asked, "One of Grandfather's 6 E's is ethics, isn't it?" His father smiled and nodded his head. When Jimmy explained to his grandfather about his apologies to his customers and the department store manager, his grandfather seemed very pleased.

The next day Jimmy opened his blue notebook and wrote "Ethics: Be open and honest."

Ethics:

Be open and
honest.

P.S. Running a
business is
hard sometimes.

As the summer went on, Jimmy's business was doing very well. He was very pleased that he now knew 5 of his grandfather's 6 E's.

Jimmy kept remembering that the sign on his grandfather's wall read 6 E's. He thought a lot about the 6th E. Jimmy kept waiting for something else to happen so he could learn the E. Jimmy went back through his little blue notebook to look at each E that he had learned by running the stand. He decided to write them down so he could look at the entire list.

6 E's

Excellence	*have a good product to sell*
Equity	*be fair to all your customers*
Effort	*work hard at your business*
Efficiency	*watch your costs*
Ethics	*be open and honest*

Jimmy thought a lot about the final E

Jimmy wrote down a 6th E but as hard as he thought, he couldn't come up with a word he was sure about. Jimmy began to think about E words. He thought of enthusiasm, eagerness, easy and energy. He showed his new list of words to his grandmother. She asked him if he had looked the words up in the dictionary. Jimmy nodded yes but he said they were all possible E's. After running the juice stand, Jimmy was sure that easy was not one of the 6 E's. They both laughed about the word, easy, and agreed it was probably not an E on the list. Grandfather entered the room while they were laughing and wondered what was so funny. Jimmy and his grandmother smiled and said it was their secret.

It was almost time for Jimmy to close his stand and start back to school. He knew his classmates would want to know about the 6 E's of successful businesses. He called Teri, his grandfather's assistant, and made an appointment to talk about the last E. He told him about the words enthusiasm, energy, and eagerness. "Jimmy, I am very pleased you are searching for the final E. Sometimes in our search for things we learn a lot along the way. Enthusiasm is good for any business. Energy and enthusiasm put together would be great. Eagerness in business is good if you don't move too quickly.

Jimmy was excited to hear that his grandfather liked the words. "But which one is the final E?" He wanted to know. His grandfather turned slowly and looked at the chart entitled 6 E's. "The words energy, enthusiasm, and eagerness are good words but they are not on the list of 6 E's of Wise Management."

Jimmy was very frustrated as he left his grandfather. He stopped by his dad's office to get a ride home. While he was waiting, he noticed a stack of booklets his father's secretary was putting together. Jimmy waited quietly for his father to come back from his meeting. Anna, his father's secretary, teased him about being a big businessman himself. "Maybe you would enjoy reading this thick company report," she laughed.

Jimmy took the heavy report and opened it. The report was filled with big words and lots of numbers that were hard to understand. When his father's meeting finished, he put the report in his backpack.

The next day when he looked in his backpack for his notebook and pencil, he noticed the report. He thought to himself, "This is for grownups," and put it in his garbage

Jimmy retrieved the company report and studied it more deeply

can. Later in the day he began to worry about the report he had put in the trash. "Maybe throwing it away might have something to do with ethics," he thought. He decided to search through the empty juice cups for the report. He tried to read the report again. This time something caught his eye. The report had a part for each one of the E's, Jimmy had discovered. Jimmy studied the report; he realized that the report was a way of measuring excellence, equity, efficiency, effort, and ethics.

That night Jimmy gave his father the booklet. "Thanks," his father said. "This is a very important report. This report tells us how we are doing with each one of the E's. This effectiveness report is our ruler, a measuring stick for National Beverage Corporation," his father said.

Jimmy creates his own effective report

"You should be pleased to have discovered the last E, effectiveness. I thought about it a long time when I ran the juice stand," he went on. Jimmy realized how lucky he was that he had discovered the 6th E almost by accident. "Sometimes the most obvious things are the hardest to learn," he thought to himself. Good luck might be helpful when you have your own business.

Jimmy decided to do his own effectiveness report for his juice stand. Jimmy made up some questions on a sheet that he gave each of his customers to complete.

After one week, he totaled up the results. He wrote at the top of a sheet in his notebook.

Jimmy's Juice Stand Effectiveness Report

"People liked my juice so the juice was *excellent*. I had a good product to sell. People thought they had been treated fairly, so there was *equity*. People thought that my price was fair. I kept the costs down enough to keep the same price for three summers."

Jimmy showed his effectiveness report to his Uncle Barry, the company business manager. His uncle was impressed, but he told Jimmy to total up all his costs for the three summers. He asked Jimmy if he had the total number of cups that he had sold. Jimmy showed him his notebook with the number of cups sold. The next day Jimmy totaled up the expenses and divided them by the cups sold. He wrote in his effectiveness report that, except for the second summer when he ran out of supplies, he had held the costs down. "Most of the time, I kept costs low so my business was *efficient*. I invested effort to repair and clean up the stand when it got run down. In addition, I was always open at 10:00 a.m. so that counts for *effort*. Once I understood what ethics were, I was careful to be open and honest in running my stand." His Uncle Barry suggested he write, "Prepared for Grandfather and submitted by his grandson, Jimmy."

He showed his grandmother the report when his mother and grandfather were at the mall looking for a birthday present for Elizabeth, his younger sister. "You must show this report to your grandfather. He will be very pleased," she said. When his grandfather came back with a present, he sat down on a bench in the mall. He read the report and gave Jimmy a big hug. "I am very proud of you for this excellent report," he said. "You have learned how to use the 6E's."

Jimmy felt very good. He liked the praise. He realized his grandfather used a lot of praise with people in the company. He was concerned that he had been lucky in discovering the final E almost by accident. "Luck seems to come to good businessmen who work hard," his grandfather said.

Jimmy was pleased because now he knew the last E. He wrote in the notebook "Effectiveness: Measure results. Sometimes it helps to be lucky."

Jimmy was very excited about going into the seventh grade. Seventh grade was different because Jimmy had a different teacher for every class. Jimmy was disappointed that his homeroom teacher, Miss Elder, had not asked Jimmy about the 6 E's. One day at homeroom he was surprised to see Miss Largent, Mr. Baxter, and Miss

Jimmy was eager to share all 6E's at school

Elder all waiting for him. They explained that Jimmy's grandfather had invited the fifth, sixth, and seventh grade classes to National Beverage Corporation for an all-day field trip. The teachers had asked the school principal, Mr. Drum, to discuss this field trip with them and Jimmy.

Mr. Drum looked over his glasses at Jimmy as he thought about the upcoming trip. Mr. Drum said he would approve the trip under one condition. He asked Jimmy if he knew what that condition would be. Jimmy thought long and hard about the question. He finally answered. "Every one of us must behave and be polite and represent Hotchkiss Middle School well." Jimmy knew that Mr. Drum was proud of his school because he always mentioned in his opening of school speech that every student was responsible for Hotchkiss Middle School's reputation. Miss Largent, Mr. Baxter, Miss Elder, and Principal Drum all broke out laughing. Jimmy was surprised. He must have really been off base with his answer. Mr. Drum said, "Your answer was great, and yes, we will expect all three classes of students to behave and be polite as they meet your grandfather and his workers on this trip. "But," he said, "I want to have you make a presentation on the 6 E's I have heard so much about from your classmates and teachers." Jimmy thought about how excited all his friends would be to go on an all-day trip. He would be very proud of his father, aunts, uncles, and his grandfather. He told Mr. Drum that he would be glad to do a talk on the 6 E's.

Mr. Drum telephoned Jimmy's grandfather to accept the invitation to tour the company. He said that they were expecting Jimmy to do a talk on the 6 E's.

Jimmy could tell that his grandfather was pleased that his grandson had been asked to speak to all the classes. Jimmy was worried about speaking to such a large group but his grandfather said talking to groups is easy when you know your subject. Jimmy knew about the 6 E's but he was not sure if he knew exactly what each one meant.

Jimmy's Uncle Derek, the public relations director for National Beverage Corporation, came to Hotchkiss Middle School during homeroom and met with all the classes to develop an itinerary for the trip. He had the students look up the word "itinerary" in the dictionary. They learned that "itinerary" meant a detailed outline for their field trip. Representatives of the three classes wrote the plan and shared it with their teachers. When Mr. Drum saw the plan he was pleased but laughed when he saw brownies and ice cream on the itinerary at the end of the day. Mr. Drum showed Jimmy a paper that Mr. Baxter,

Miss Largent, and Miss Elder had written. He wanted to know what the students were going to learn.

Learning Outcomes
1. How are beverages made? *(production)*
2. How are beverages delivered? *(distribution)*
3. How are beverages sold? *(marketing)*
4. What are the company's 6 E's? *(values)*

Jimmy's schoolmates were excited to see beverages being mixed. They were impressed with all the different cans, bottles, and packages the National Beverage Corporation used. Jimmy's friends liked the big shiny trucks that lined the docks where workers loaded the products to be taken to areas all across the country. Jimmy's grandfather stayed with Jimmy's class throughout the tour. They tasted all kinds of juice at almost every stop. When they got to the big meeting room for lunch, Jimmy was surprised to see all of his grandfather's managers and vice presidents there to eat with the students.

Jimmy's grandfather stepped forward and thanked the teachers, Mr. Drum, and all the students for coming.

He said he appreciated his management team joining with the students for lunch. He asked the students to think of things they could tell their parents about what they had learned. They named several things they had seen on the trip. Each student wrote down three learning outcomes they could share when they went home.

After a great lunch with all sorts of things that students liked, Jimmy's grandfather introduced Jimmy to give his presentation on the 6 E's. Jimmy was very nervous in front of all the students. But, in addition, he had certainly not planned on the National Beverage Corporation management team being there.

Jimmy explained what he had learned from the three summers

Jimmy carefully explained what he had learned over the three summers running his juice stand. He had a cardboard sign he placed on an easel. He had written what he had learned. He explained what each E meant.

6 E's

Excellence	*have a good product to sell*
Equity	*be fair to all your customers*
Effort	*work hard at your business*
Efficiency	*watch your costs*
Ethics	*be open and honest*
Effectiveness	*measure results*

All Jimmy's classmates at Hotchkiss Middle School clapped, but his grandfather's management team clapped the loudest. When the applause stopped, Jimmy's grandfather brought out another easel covered with a white cloth. "Let's see if Jimmy's 6 E's are the same as National Beverage Corporation's 6 E's," he said. Then he quickly uncovered the sign.

The 6 E's Model for Success

Excellence	*maintain quality control of products*
Equity	*treat customers with impartiality and fairness*
Effort	*develop staff commitment to the company*
Efficiency	*insure the value of our products to clients*
Ethics	*support open, honest and fair business practice*
Effectiveness	*determine outcomes and results*

Jimmy was concerned when he looked at his grandfather's E's because maybe he had not really discovered the magical 6 E's. His grandfather was smiling when he explained that the words may be slightly different but they meant the same. Jimmy felt good when everyone clapped. Jimmy knew that he was very lucky to have his family, his school, his teachers, and his grandfather and grandmother. Jimmy's grandfather laughed and said, "How about all of us celebrating with chocolate brownies and ice cream." Everyone was happy. Jimmy was thinking about starting his younger sister, Elizabeth, in the juice stand business the next summer.